THE Hanukkah Story

Text by Anita Ganeri 2004
Illustrations by Rachael Phillips
© copyright in this edition Tulip Books 2017

Printed in Malta by Melita Press

ISBN 978-1-78388-062-1

THE Hanukkah Story

Anita Ganeri
Illustrated by
Rachael Phillips

Contents

More than two thousand years ago, a Greek king called Antiochus ruled over a vast empire.
In every land of his empire, he ordered people to give up their own religious beliefs and to worship the Greek gods instead. Only the Jews in Israel refused to obey the king.

"Blessed is he that comes in the name of the Lord," they shouted. "Hosanna in the highest."

The Jews wanted to follow their own religion. They wanted to worship one God and no other, as their holy books had taught them to do. But King Antiochus wanted the Jews to follow Greek customs and traditions. Furious, he decided to punish the Jews and to try to destroy the Jewish religion.

King Antiochus stopped the Jews from following the teaching of the Torah, their holy book. He forbade them from keeping their holy day of rest and prayer, the Shabbat, sacred. Then he sent his soldiers to the holy city of Jerusalem.

They ransacked the Temple, the Jews' most sacred place, where they worshipped God. The soldiers stole the Temple treasures and snuffed out the special oil lamp which burned day and night as a symbol of God's presence.

A statue of the Greek
god, Zeus, was set up
in the Temple instead.
Antiochus ordered that
every Jew must sacrifice
a pig to Zeus. This was
a cruel thing to ask
because, according to
Jewish law, pigs were
considered unclean.
Anyone who refused to
obey was killed.

Even though their lives were in danger, many Jews refused to obey the king's command. But how could they fight against the Greeks when their numbers were so small?

Not far away from Jerusalem, in the small town of Modi'in, there lived an old priest called Mattathias and his five sons. Mattathias and his sons refused to make a sacrifice to the Greek gods. They pulled down statues of gods in the town, killed the soldier who read out the king's orders and fled to the nearby hills to hide. Soon, more and more Jews joined them. They wanted to stay true to God and they were ready to risk their lives for Him.

When Mattathias the priest died, one of his sons, Judah, took over command. He organised the Jews into an army to fight for freedom. When King Antiochus saw what was going on he was furious. Determined to crush the Jews once and for all, he gathered a mighty army and led them into battle against the Jews.

As the two sides lined up to fight, the small band of Jews were dismayed to see how big the Greek army was. What chance did they stand against such a great force? But Judah would not let his men become downhearted.

"The king's army is large," he told them. "But we are fighting for God. He will protect us."

In the battle that followed, Judah's army fought hard and bravely against the Greeks. Even though they were greatly outnumbered, the Jews won a great victory. It seemed that God truly was on their side, watching over them. Many more victories followed against Antiochus's forces. And, in time, the little army of Jews drove the enemy out of Jerusalem.

Triumphantly, Judah led the Jews into their holy city. They flocked to the Temple to thank God for their victory. A dreadful sight met their eyes.

"The first thing we must do," said Judah, "is repair all the damage to our sacred Temple."

The Jews took down all the images of the Greek gods. Then they set about cleaning the Temple and making it holy once more.

When they were finished, Judah said, "We must light the oil lamp's flame again to celebrate our victory. Then the Temple will belong to God once more."

But when the Jews looked for oil to light the lamp, they saw that every jar of oil in the Temple had been broken.

Suddenly, Judah spotted a jar hidden in a corner, but the jar had only enough to keep the lamp burning for a single day. It would take eight days for Judah's men to fetch more. Whatever was Judah to do?

Judah lit the lamp. To his amazement it did not go out at the end of the day. Instead it kept burning the next day, and the next, and the day after that. In fact, it kept burning for eight whole days, long enough for the Jews to fetch fresh supplies of oil. A great miracle had happened.

Since that time, Jewish people have celebrated the festival of Hanukkah. They light lamps to remember the miracle that happened in the Temple long ago. They remember how God showed them that he was always with them and how they won the freedom to worship Him.

The Hanukkah Lamp

At the festival of Hanukkah, Jews look back at this special time in their history and remember God's great miracle. They light eight candles on a special candlestick, one on the first night of Hanukkah, two on the second, and so on until all eight are lit. The ninth candle, in the centre, is used for lighting

the others. Before lighting each candle, special prayers and blessings are said.

In the time of Judah, however, the Hanukkah candlestick only had seven candles. Hanukkah, the festival of lights, usually takes place in December.

The Meaning of Hanukkah

The story of Hanukkah is all about people sticking to their own beliefs and values, even when this puts their lives in danger. The Jews did not want to be forced to stop being themselves or to give up God's commandments. The story teaches that being different is not easy. But sometimes it is more important to stand up for what you believe than to accept what you do not believe.

A Hanukkah Recipe

At Hanukkah, people eat food fried in oil to remember the miracle of the oil in the Temple lamp. Here you can find out how to make your own tasty potato latkes (pancakes) for Hanukkah.

ASK AN ADULT TO HELP YOU

Ingredients:

6 medium potatoes

1 medium onion, 2 eggs

2 tablespoons plain flour

1 teaspoon baking powder

salt and pepper, oil for frying

What to do:

1. Peel and grate the potatoes. Squeeze as much water out of them as possible.
2. Beat the eggs and add them to the potatoes, with the other ingredients.
3. With an adult's help, heat the oil in a frying pan.
4. Drop spoonfuls of the mixture into the oil. Flatten each pancake with the spoon.
5. Fry the pancakes on each side until they are brown and crispy.
6. Drain the pancakes on kitchen paper and serve them hot with apple sauce or sour cream.

Playing Dreidel

Join in the fun of Hanukkah and play dreidel. The game began when the Jews were ruled by the Syrian Greeks. They were forbidden to read the Torah, their holy book, so they had to study it secretly. If they were caught, they quickly hid their books and began to play dreidel instead.

You will need:

a dreidel

(A dreidel is a spinning top with four sides. Each side is marked with a Hebrew letter. The letters stand for the words 'Nes, Gadol, Hayah, Sham' which mean 'A great miracle happened here'.)

a pile of counters, chocolate coins or raisins

(Each player starts with the same number of counters.)

How to play:

1. Each player puts a counter in the middle.
2. Everyone takes it in turns to spin the dreidel.
If it lands with this letter facing upwards:
(Nun) You do Nothing
(Gimmel) You Grab everything in the middle
(Hey) You take Half of the counters
(Shin) You Shove another counter in
3. After each player's go, everyone puts another counter in.
4. The winner is the person who gets all the counters.